Jesús, He es...

BOOK 1

"...the way, the truth and the life. No one comes to the
Father except through me."
John 14:6

MARITZA RIVERA

JESUS, HE IS...
MARITZA RIVERA
BOOK 1

FRONT COVER: DIEZ VECES MÁS GROUP
DIEZVECESMAS@GMAIL.COM
LAYOUT: ANAMARIA TORELLI DE GELL
TRADUCTER : ELMER GARCÍA URZUA
ELMER@ILOVEJESUS.NET

FIRST EDITION
SEPTIEMBRE 2022

CONTACTS :
MSMARZA123@GMAIL.COM
1(347)613.5690

ORDERS:
AMAZON.COM
AMAZON.ES
AMAZON.MEX

Acknowledgements

I would first like to thank the One who inspired me to write this book, my beloved Heavenly Father, Lord Jesus, and precious and powerful Holy Spirit. Thank you for entrusting me with the great privilege of making me yours.

Secondly, I want to thank all my family for always being there for me and blessing, supporting, and encouraging me.

I also want to thank the entire sisterhood for their unconditional support and believing in me.

And infinite thanks to you, who decided to read and study this book designed to help you grow and learn more about the work of Jesus Christ in your life.

May God richly bless you always!

Foreword

I love the way this book is structured. It flows through Biblical concepts so evenly with a simple language, that makes understanding it so easy.
Tony Ramírez/ Actuario

One of the reasons many people judge God is because they don't know Him. But when we delve deeper into who He is, we get to know Him in His different manifestations resulting in maturity, growth, and confidence in Him. One of the themes from the book that struck me was the one on fasting, especially when comparing how we see it and how God sees it. The book is very edifying, and I believe it fills a great need for information and revelation in the Body of Christ.
Psalmist Raquel Amparo

This precious book, Jesus He is... is a very practical manual designed to help us share God's pure word effectively, both to believers and non-believers alike. It has a clear language that allows us to learn to pray through the word and fast according to GOD's teachings, leading us to discover the FATHER'S purpose for our lives.
Martha Lucía Vallejo
Director of Sirviendo con Amor Ministries
Pereira, Colombia

It's an anointed book, that certainly emanates from the heart of God, with a clear and simple language that never loses the depth of the revelation received from Him. I strongly recommend its reading at any level.

Pastor Maximo Reyes Forchue
Adulam de Juda International Ministries
Santo Domingo, Dominican Republic

I find the inspiration God gave Prophet Maritza Rivera for writing this book quite interesting. And I personally believe it will serve as a blessed tool in the lives of many new believers who wish to strengthen their roots in our Christian faith. I have known Prophet Maritza for many years, and I believe the Holy Spirit has inspired this work to bless many.

Apostol Benjamin Ascencio
King Jesus Ministries Honduras

Studying a book is always challenging, a blessing, and very enriching, but it is also nice to know about the author.
I recommend this literary work which will surely be an added blessing to every reader's life. Blessings!

Pastor and Author
Reverend Libia Gutierrez
Panama

Maritza's relentless passion to see many others grow in their Christian faith has led to this special book of Jesus, He is... Her special grace to share powerful Biblical foundations in such a simple, easy-to-understand and applicable way is sure to impact your life and create new inroads in your Christian walk. I was greatly blessed by the anointing on this book, as I know you will too!

Elmer Garcia
Minister and interpreter
Casa De Dios Guatemala

Jesus, He is...is a wonderful and precise book with excellent content, written with simplicity without losing its depth. This book is sure to save you years of questions if you are just beginning to know the King of Kings, and you have a Bible and friends with whom to share and talk about God's redemptive work. The next step will be to continue reading here...

Prophet Simon Aquino
Chile

Introduction

The book '***Jesus, He is***' is a very suitable, entry-level manual to evangelize and disciple people. It is geared towards all those who know nothing about the Word of God, nor have ever been a part of God's church, and for people of different spiritual levels and backgrounds. This manual is designed to help them read the Bible. Moreover, I can assure you that this book will spiritually refresh and renew your relationship with God.

I have written and explained it in a simple manner, based on the foundations of the Christian faith, with very specific Bible verses. Every subject is based solely on the Word of God and not on any personal opinions, religious groups, or any given denomination.

I have made sure to include the information on each subject that your Heavenly Father wants you to know of His Person and the immense love that his beloved Son Jesus has for you. Also, that you may come to know the divine person of the Holy Spirit since all three of them are one. His guidance has inspired this entire work.

I can assure you that by the end of this experience, your life will be transformed and infused with an impartation of his precious Holy Spirit. He is the one who is going to fill you with the knowledge and revelation of each of the twenty subjects covered in this book.

Another benefit of reading this work is discovering your divine purpose and origin. I also provide you with many tools to dramatically grow your faith so that you can pray and fast powerfully and effectively according to the Lord's true fast.

As you study this book, you will come to know the priceless value of our Lord Jesus Christ's sacrifice on the cross of Calvary and His exceedingly powerful resurrection that ushers the hope of eternal life into our lives as we grow in our glorious relationship with Him.

I would like to close these words with a personal testimony.

I was going through a very challenging health crisis in my life, incapacitated for months. Yet, it was during that difficult time when I received the exciting mission to create this discipleship manual, an easy and straightforward handbook that one can also use to evangelize and carry out the Great Commission as set forth in Matthew 28:19,
"Go therefore and make disciples of all the nations, baptizing them in the name of the Father and of the Son and of the Holy Spirit."

I have prayed for these teachings to be a powerful blessing for every person that longs to know more about God; and it is my heartfelt desire to collaborate with every one of our Heavenly Father's ministers and workers to build the church of our Lord Jesus Christ. My one and only goal is to make His holy gospel known evermore and for the Word of God to reach every corner of the globe.

I truly hope you enjoy it as much as I did!

Index

1

Our Heavenly Father

GETTING TO KNOW OUR ORIGIN AND CREATOR

Today is the day for you to come to know the Heavenly Father as our creator. I tell you that He is the one who formed and designed us before ever creating the universe and everything that exists.

- He was the one who thought us and planned us out.

- It was He, also, who placed us in our mother's womb.

The scriptures say in Psalms 139:13
"For You formed my inward parts;
You covered me in my mother's womb."

And verse 16 says:
"Your eyes saw my substance, being yet unformed.
And in Your book they all were written, the days
fashioned for me, when as yet there were none of them."

- It is so wonderful to know that God is the great creator. He thought us out and then made us in His image and likeness, exclusively, to enter into a relationship with us, as His children.

- We are not orphans or bastards, but we are God's beloved children. Yes, those of us who have received Him, are His perfect and supreme creation. The Bible calls us "the crown of His creation," making us male and female.

Notice how the following verses confirm these truths:

Jeremiah 1:4-10

4 Then the word of the Lord came to me, saying:
5 "Before I formed you in the womb, I knew you;
Before you were born, I sanctified you. I ordained you a prophet to the nations."
6 Then said I: "Ah, Lord God!
Behold, I cannot speak, for I am a youth."
7 But the Lord said to me: "Do not say, 'I am a youth,'
For you shall go to all to whom I send you,
And whatever I command you, you shall speak.
8 Do not be afraid of their faces, for I am with you to deliver you," says the Lord.
9 Then the Lord put forth His hand and touched my mouth, and the Lord said to me: "Behold, I have put My words in your mouth.
10 See, I have this day set you over the nations and over the kingdoms, to root out and to pull down, to destroy and to throw down, to build and to plant."

- God was right there watching over you the day you were born, with a powerful assignment in mind, a destiny for your life.

- God is the Father who keeps our lives and all our ways. We are his creation.

Ephesians 2:10 says,
"For we are His workmanship, created in Christ Jesus for good works, which God prepared beforehand that we should walk in them."

Genesis 1:27 says the following,
"So, God created man in His own image; in the image of God, He created him; male and female He created them."

And **Psalms 33:6** says that,
"By the word of the Lord the heavens were made, and all the host of them by the breath of His mouth."

- It is such an amazing privilege to have been fashioned by the hands of our Heavenly Father Himself and made into His image and likeness!!

- God made us; therefore, we belong to Him alone.

Genesis 1:26
Then God said, "Let Us make man in Our image, according to Our likeness; let them have dominion over the fish of the sea, over the birds of the air, and over the cattle, over all the earth and over every creeping thing that creeps on the earth."

Do you see now that He created us with a purpose, to have power and dominion to rule over all creation!

- We are the ones, as created human beings, whose assignment is to rule over all creation and not creation over us.

- There is no doubt that all human beings are descendants of God. We do not come from monkeys, nor are we the product of any type of evolution. The Bible clearly states this.

Ecclesiastes 3:11 says,
"He has made everything beautiful in its time. Also, He has put eternity in their hearts, except that no one can find out the work that God does from beginning to end."

- This is why we know that God is not finished with you or me, yet. We know it because His Word says that He continues perfecting His plan and destiny in us.

- He Himself is revealing His plan and purpose in us, and the closer we get to Him, the more we discover it.

- When He formed us, the Creator gave each one of us a purpose, abilities, and talents.

- God also gave us a prophetic destiny: a work to complete here on earth. We came into this world with goals and purposes already set by Him, prepared beforehand and designed in advance by our loving Heavenly Father just for us.

Nonetheless, God, the Father, is so patient and merciful with all of us, helping us fulfill our prophetic destiny daily through His powerful Holy Spirit.

- Our Heavenly Father guides and directs us, and He teaches us how to be true children of His.

- God has a precise time to manifest Himself to every person. He is never late. He expects us to recognize that we are the true children of the Light, able to manifest ourselves to carry out His perfect will.

In **Romans 8:1,** God tells us how He wants us to reveal His light and manifest His love, glory, and life:

"For the earnest expectation of the creation eagerly waits for the manifestation of the sons of God."

- Manifestation means to display or show the world that we are the sons of the Father of lights. In him, there is no darkness, no shadow of variation; in God, there is no evil.

I want to encourage you to get to know this loving and faithful Father. All He wants is to bless us with every heavenly and earthly blessing in Christ Jesus, His beloved Son.

GOD'S ATTRIBUTES AND CHARACTER

Getting to know God's attributes.

Each one of them is blended in perfect unity, and all together form the remarkable character of the living God. As we mention the Father's traits and features, we will also realize how his Son Jesus and the Holy Spirit are one in themselves as well. In other words, these attributes are common to the Godhead, all belonging to the Father, the Son, and the Holy Spirit.

Let's begin with the first attribute.

- **GOD IS OMNIPRESENT:**

He is everywhere. There is no place that he cannot dwell.

1 Reyes 8:27

"But will God indeed dwell on the earth? Behold, heaven and the heaven of heavens cannot contain You. How much less this temple which I have built!"
Psalms 139:7-12
7 Where can I go from Your Spirit?
Or where can I flee from Your presence?
8 If I ascend into heaven, You are there;
If I make my bed in hell, behold, You are there.
9 If I take the wings of the morning,
And dwell in the uttermost parts of the sea,
10 Even there Your hand shall lead me,
And Your right hand shall hold me.
11 If I say, "Surely the darkness shall fall on me,"
Even the night shall be light about me;
12 Indeed, the darkness shall not hide from You,
But the night shines as the day;
The darkness and the light are both alike to You."

Proverbs 15:3

"The eyes of the Lord are in every place,
keeping watch on the evil and the good."

Isaiah 66:1

Thus says the Lord: "Heaven is My throne, and earth is My footstool. Where is the house that you will build Me? And where is the place of My rest?"

Job 34:21

"For His eyes are on the ways of man, and He sees all his steps."

- **GOD IS OMNISCIENT (ALL-KNOWING).**
He knows all and sees all. His knowledge is limitless.

Matthew 10:29-30
29 "Are not two sparrows sold for a copper coin? And not one of them falls to the ground apart from your Father's will.

30 But the very hairs of your head are all numbered."

Job 34:21-22
21 "For His eyes are on the ways of man, and He sees all his steps.

22 There is no darkness nor shadow of death where the workers of iniquity may hide themselves."

Psalms 147:5
"Great is our Lord, and mighty in power; His understanding is infinite."

Hebrews 4:13
13 "And there is no creature hidden from His sight, but all things are naked and open to the eyes of Him to whom we must give account."

- **GOD IS OMNIPOTENT:**
He is all powerful. All power is in His Hands. He is known as the One who can do all things, because NOTHING is impossible for God.

Genesis 17:1
"When Abram was ninety-nine years old, the Lord appeared to Abram and said to him, "I am the Almighty God; walk before Me and be blameless."

Exodus 6:3

I appeared to Abraham, to Isaac, and to Jacob, as God Almighty, but by My name Lord I was not known to them.

Psalms 91:1

"He who dwells in the secret place of the Most High Shall abide under the shadow of the Almighty."

- **GOD IS HOLY:**

  God is perfectly holy. There is no one as holy as Him.

Leviticus 11:44-45

44 "For I am the Lord your God. You shall therefore consecrate yourselves, and you shall be holy; for I am holy. Neither shall you defile yourselves with any creeping thing that creeps on the earth.
45 For I am the Lord who brings you up out of the land of Egypt, to be your God. You shall therefore be holy, for I am holy."

1 Peter 1:15-16

15 but as He who called you is holy, you also be holy in all your conduct,
16 because it is written, "Be holy, for I am holy."

1 Samuel 2:2

"No one is holy like the Lord, for there is none besides You, nor is there any rock like our God."

Isaiah 5:16 (NLT)

"But the Lord of Heaven's Armies will be exalted by his justice. The holiness of God will be displayed by his righteousness."

DESCRIBING SOME OF GOD'S NAMES AND THEIR MEANINGS.

It is very important that as we get to know our Father, we also learn some of God's more widely-known names —those by which He has made Himself known. We must also understand why we should call on Him by His different names in the various circumstances in which He manifests Himself.

- God's names define His essence, His nature, His personality, as well as His character and His role.

We see this in the book of Exodus chapter 3 and verses 13-15:

13 Then Moses said to God, "Indeed, when I come to the children of Israel and say to them, 'The God of your fathers has sent me to you,' and they say to me, 'What is His name?' what shall I say to them?"

14 And God said to Moses, "I AM WHO I AM." And He said, "Thus you shall say to the children of Israel, 'I AM has sent me to you.' "

15 Moreover God said to Moses, "Thus you shall say to the children of Israel: 'The Lord God of your fathers, the God of Abraham, the God of Isaac, and the God of Jacob, has sent me to you. This is My name forever, and this is My memorial to all generations.'"

In response to Moses' insistence on wanting to know God's name, He answered him like this: "I Am Who I Am." Moreover, God commanded Moses to: "Tell this to the Israelites: The Lord, the God of their ancestors."

Thus, we can say that this is God's true name: "The Lord, I am Who I Am."

Additional Names of God

- El **Shaddai**: means the almighty God. He used it when he appeared to Abraham, Isaac, and Jacob.

Exodus 6:2-3
2 And God spoke to Moses and said to him: "I am the Lord.
3 I appeared to Abraham, to Isaac, and to Jacob, as God Almighty, but by My name Lord I was not known to them."

God the Father is infinite in His character, and there are two other names that also reflect this attribute:

- **Elohim**: which is the same as "God," and means "the unique God," "Creator," and comes from the Hebrew word Elohim = "the God of gods".

Genesis 1:1
"In the beginning God created the heavens and the earth."

The name YHWH, it seems, is written solely with consonants and refers to "Yahweh" = I Am who I Am, the Lord! It is also the most commonly used name in all scripture.

- The Tetragrammaton, **YHWH**, transliterated from the Hebrew, means that God is present and attentive to every event and circumstance. It can also be read as "Jehovah."

- **Adonai** comes from the Hebrew root word Adon meaning "lord and master."

Genesis 14:19-20

19 And he blessed him and said: "Blessed be Abram of God Most High, Possessor of heaven and earth;
20 And blessed be God Most High, Who has delivered your enemies into your hand."

- El **Elyon** means "the God that is higher than any other god."

There are many other names and roles of God, and you will be able to discover them later on as you get to know the Scriptures.

QUESTIONNAIRE

Exercise 1: Fill in the blanks with the words from the box:

> Image covered. Womb. eyes. fashioned. Orphans. Formed. Children. Womb. Bastards. Prophet. Formed. Man.

1. Psalms 139:13 "For You _____ my inward parts; You _____ me in my mother's _____."

2. "Your _____ saw my substance, being yet unformed. And in Your book, they all were written, the days _____ for me, when as yet there were none of them."

3. We are not _____, nor are we _____ but His beloved _____.

4. Jeremiah 1:4-5 "Then the word of the Lord came to me, saying: Before I _____ you in the _____ I knew you. Before you were born, I sanctified you; I ordained you a _____ to the nations."

5. Genesis 1:27 "So God created _____ in His own

image; in the _____ of God He created him; male and female He created them."

Exercise 2: Fill in the blank with the correct name of God.

Adonai. Shaddai. Yahweh. Elohim. El Elyon.

1. I am who I am: _____

2. The unique God, Creator: _____

3. The Almighty God:_____

4. Lord and Master: _____

5. Most High God:_____

Exercise 3: Complete each phrase or verse with the correct word.

1. We are not orphans or bastards but the beloved children of _____.

2. Ephesians 2:10 says, "For we are His workmanship, created in _____ for good works."

3. God is everywhere. There is nowhere He cannot be because He is _____.

4. God knows all things, and He sees all things. His wisdom has no limits. He is _____.

5. God is almighty. All power belongs to Him. He is known as the God who "can do all things," because nothing is impossible for Him. He is _____.

6. Leviticus 11:44 says, "For I am the Lord your God. You shall therefore consecrate yourselves, and you shall be holy; for I am _____."

7. Isaiah 5:16 says, "But the Lord of _____ shall be exalted in judgment, and God who is holy shall be hallowed in righteousness.

8. Exodus 3:13 and 14a says, "...and they say to me, 'What is His name?' what shall I say to them?" And God said to Moses, "I _____."

2

Jesus Christ

JESUS, HE IS THE GREATEST LOVE!

Now, I will show you a little more of the Father's love through his only begotten son Jesus, whom you have probably heard of so many times in many celebrations and traditional holidays. An example of this is when part of the Christian world celebrates the birth of Jesus on December 25th.

Christmas is one of the most well-known celebrations for Christian families worldwide. Likewise, you may have also heard the name of Jesus during the celebration of Holy Week (Easter break), which commemorates His sacrifice, suffering, and death on the cross and His mighty resurrection.

Although these dates are not exact, the vast majority of us have observed them at some point in our lives.

So, let's talk about what matters most for us all to come to know God's great and perfect love through Jesus Christ.

Let's see what the Bible has to say about God's great love for us:

John 3:16
"For God so loved the world that He gave His only begotten Son, that whoever believes in Him should not perish but have everlasting life."

This passage of scripture speaks to us about a vast and unconditional love.

- God loves every creature He made. God longs to have a genuine Father-son relationship with us and establish His loving fatherhood and a family. That is why He gave us His son Jesus Christ to come down to earth. Leaving his glorious and heavenly throne, Jesus came down, became a man, and died for us all.

- When Jesus became a man, he stripped Himself of all his glory and majesty and offered himself as "The Lamb of God who takes away the sin of the world."

Philippians 2:7
"...but made Himself of no reputation, taking the form of a bondservant, and coming in the likeness of men."

- **Jesus, He is** the One who, for our sake, endured all the suffering on the cross in obedience to the Father.

We speak of the fact that while being God, Jesus Christ became man to fulfill his mission.

Matthew 1:18

"Now the birth of Jesus Christ was as follows: After His mother Mary was betrothed to Joseph, before they came together, she was found with child of the Holy Spirit."

- **Jesus, He is** the one whom the Holy Spirit begot in a young virgin named Mary. In other words, his birth was a miraculous, divine work.

- **Jesus, He is** the One who offered Himself as a " Sacrificial Lamb" without sin or blemish. He is the One who paid the price for our sins with His death, allowing Himself to be slain on the cross. He is the One who suffered unto death, out of love, to keep us from being separated forevermore from the Father. Our savior suffered beatings and humiliations, finally shedding all his precious blood for your sake and that of all humankind.

Matthew 20:19

"...and deliver Him to the Gentiles to mock and to scourge and to crucify. And the third day He will rise again."

WHY AND HOW WAS JESUS SACRIFICED?

- **John 15:13** says that He did so willingly:
"Greater love has no one than this, than to lay down one's life for his friends."

- His purpose in becoming a man and dying on the cross is that none of us should perish but have everlasting life.

The Son of God came down to earth to be and dwell in constant relationship with the Father's children. He offered Himself as a ransom that we might live in this world in peace, free of fear and loving our heavenly Father, the Maker of all men.

Luke 9:24

"For whoever desires to save his life will lose it, but whoever loses his life for My sake will save it."

- Jesus, He is the One who paid our sinful debt so that we might have eternal life and live with the assurance of a victorious life.

- Jesus, He is the One who gave it all for us and restored our entry back to the throne of grace, to enjoy a true and direct relationship with God and free access into His presence.

Titus 2:14

"...who gave Himself for us, that He might redeem us from every lawless deed and purify for Himself His own special people, zealous for good works."

- **Jesus, He is** the One who died that we might live a full, plentiful life filled with the glory of His majestic presence. Through Him, we are filled with His peace and abundant power.

It is in this new life provided by Christ Jesus that we find faith and hope for a better and blessed destiny with an eternal purpose and a glorious future, built and designed by our Heavenly Father, Himself.

- **Jesus, He is** the One who desires that you genuinely receive Him into your life and believe that He came to die for you and redeem and rescue you from the miry clay and all the rebellion and sin we walk in when we are without Christ.

- **Jesus, He** is the Savior who wants to pull you out of the pit of despair, free you from every vice and chain of ungodliness, and spare you from bad friendships and decisions that can lead your life to ruin.

- **Jesus, He** is the One who saves you from poverty and misery and delivers you from the curse of sickness.

Read **Isaiah 53**.

In addition to the above, Jesus is the one who came to deliver you from the second death. It is no longer a physical one but the one that condemns you to an eternity outside of heaven, far from God and His kingdom.

- **Jesus, He is** the One who came to cleanse you from every impurity (iniquity,) wickedness, rebellion, transgression, and every bondage and evil dealing in the world that want to keep you in captivity.

- **Jesus, He is** the One who gave Himself to set you free from every spiritual enslavement, for He alone took captivity captive when He descended into the depths of hell.

   He did it for you and all of us.

- **Jesus, He is** the One who heals, binds and makes your wounds whole.

I recommend reading Isaiah 61.

- "Jesus has seated us in heavenly places together with Him," according to Ephesians 2:6.

- **Jesus, He is** the One who snatched the keys of death and Hades from the devil (Revelation 1:18) and handed them over to His Church, which is us, His children, to you and me! To give us power and authority in this life.

We have complete authority from God to undo all the works of darkness, especially the enemy's plan against the souls of men. It is then that we will be able to live victorious lives in Him.

Isaiah 53:1-12

1 "Who has believed our report? And to whom has the arm of the Lord been revealed?

2 For He shall grow up before Him as a tender plant, and as a root out of dry ground. He has no form or comeliness; and when we see Him, there is no beauty that we should desire Him.

3 He is despised and rejected by men, a Man of sorrows and acquainted with grief. And we hid, as it were, our faces from Him; He was despised, and we did not esteem Him.

4 Surely He has borne our griefs and carried our sorrows; Yet we esteemed Him stricken, smitten by God, and afflicted.

5 But He was wounded for our transgressions, He was bruised for our iniquities; the chastisement for our peace was upon Him, and by His stripes we are healed.

6 All we like sheep have gone astray; we have turned,

every one, to his own way; and the Lord has laid on Him the iniquity of us all.

7 He was oppressed, and He was afflicted, yet He opened not His mouth. He was led as a lamb to the slaughter and as a sheep before its shearers is silent,
so He opened not His mouth.

8 He was taken from prison and from judgment, and who will declare His generation? For He was cut off from the land of the living, for the transgressions of My people He was stricken.

9 And they made His grave with the wicked —but with the rich at His death, because He had done no violence nor was any deceit in His mouth.

10 Yet it pleased the Lord to bruise Him. He has put Him to grief. When You make His soul an offering for sin, He shall see His seed, He shall prolong His days and the pleasure of the Lord shall prosper in His hand.

11 He shall see the labor of His soul, and be satisfied.
By His knowledge My righteous Servant shall justify many, for He shall bear their iniquities.

12 Therefore, I will divide Him a portion with the great, and He shall divide the spoil with the strong, because He poured out His soul unto death, and He was numbered with the transgressors, and He bore the sin of many, and made intercession for the transgressors."

- **Jesus, He is t**he Resurrection and the Life!

John 11:25

"Jesus said to her, 'I am the resurrection and the life. He who believes in Me, though he may die, he shall live.'"

- **Jesus, He is** the One who rose again from the grave on the third day. Notice what an angel said at the tomb when they came to look for Him.

Mark 16:6

"But he said to them, "Do not be alarmed. You seek Jesus of Nazareth, who was crucified. He is risen! He is not here. See the place where they laid Him."

Matthew 28:5-6

5 "But the angel answered and said to the women, 'Do not be afraid, for I know that you seek Jesus who was crucified.

6 He is not here; for He is risen, as He said. Come, see the place where the Lord lay.'"

1 Corinthians 15:3-6

3 For I delivered to you first of all that which I also received: that Christ died for our sins according to the Scriptures,

4 and that He was buried, and that He rose again the third day according to the Scriptures,

5 and that He was seen by Cephas, then by the twelve.

6 After that He was seen by over five hundred brethren at once, of whom the greater part remain to the present, but some have fallen asleep."

- **Jesus, He is** "The way, the truth and the life." And no one can come unto the Father except through Him. -John 14:6

- **Jesus, He is** the only way to our Heavenly Father. He is the only mediator between God and man.

1 Timothy 2:5

"For there is one God and one Mediator between God and men, the Man Christ Jesus..."

- **Jesus, He is** the Bread and the Water of Life.

John 6:51
"I am the living bread which came down from heaven. If anyone eats of this bread, he will live forever; and the bread that I shall give is My flesh, which I shall give for the life of the world."

In **John 6:55** Jesus says: "And Jesus said to them, 'I am the bread of life. He who comes to Me shall never hunger, and he who believes in Me shall never thirst.'"

Jesus gives us a powerful revelation of His divine person!

- If we choose to always eat of His flesh and believe in Him, He promises that we will never thirst again. Because Jesus is the water of life.

John 4:14
"But whoever drinks of the water that I shall give him will never thirst. But the water that I shall give him will become in him a fountain of water springing up into everlasting life."

Living waters can be defined as:

- It is water that flows and becomes oxygenated. The waters of the Holy Spirit flow through our entire being, making us feel His precious Presence.

- It is the assurance that we are filled with His Spirit, which gives us life and imbues us with His power and love.

- Those living waters can be likened to those that spring from the depths of the earth, pure and crystalline waters free of any contaminant.

- Living waters are always in constant movement. They can never remain stagnant; otherwise, they lose their oxygen and start to decay.

Jeremiah 2:14
"For My people have committed two evils: they have forsaken Me, the fountain of living waters and hewn themselves cisterns—broken cisterns that can hold no water."

We must be people who are wise and full of understanding.

We recognize that Jesus is...

- The Gift of God. -John 4:10

- The one who said: "My food is to do the will of Him who sent Me, and to finish His work." -John 4:34.

- The one who also promised to grant the mysteries of His kingdom to whosoever keeps His commandments (Matthew 13:11) and to be a spring of living waters that gush forth unto everlasting life (John 4:14).

Such a remarkable promise, to grant us the mysteries of God's Kingdom! It is the same as receiving the most extraordinary revelations and knowledge of His Kingdom and Mysteries.

- Knowing the mysteries of the kingdom is the same as having God's intelligence and the greatest of His wisdom. And it is so that we can keep all His commandments, not just some, but all His precepts, and thus, be able to fulfill His perfect will in our lives.

- It is just so glorious! Jesus literally gives us the divine formula to be a people that are superbly blessed and possess all His knowledge and fullness.

Notice what Jesus tells his disciples before ascending to heaven!

John 14:26
"But the Helper, the Holy Spirit, whom the Father will send in My name, He will teach you all things, and bring to your remembrance all things that I said to you."

- It means that His mighty Holy Spirit will not allow us to forget His promises nor any of the words that Jesus has spoken to us.

There is so much more about the life of our Lord Jesus Christ.

I want to urge every student of this manual to read the book of John, and all the other books of the New Testament, in the Bible, where you will find the most beautiful revelations of God's love.

You will also learn more about the work and life of God's Son during His time here on Earth. And not only that, but your faith will increase as you learn about the great miracles Jesus performed throughout His time here.

The main work Jesus Christ did was to give His precious life as a ransom for our sins so that whosoever believes in Him will not perish but have everlasting life.

- We get eternal life when we receive Jesus Christ in our hearts as the Savior and Lord of our lives, and we entrust ourselves to Him so that He takes complete control of our destiny. We follow by doing His will as obedient children to His commandments and His Word.

By the end of this book, you will see that the last subject is on God's Promises and His Covenants. I can assure you that they will be exciting, and you will want to attain every last one of them.

- Through His sacrifice, Jesus redeemed and rescued us from this world where we lay hopeless, without God.

There is victory in a life in Christ Jesus our Lord!

Would you like to receive forgiveness for your sins, and give your life to be with Jesus, the Lord of your life, now?

If you say yes, then just say the following prayer:

*"Heavenly Father, I ask your forgiveness for all my sins.
I confess that I have sinned against You.
But Father, today, I repent with all my heart, and I ask you to forgive me.
Wash me in Your precious blood, and make me a new creation, a new person, free to love and forgive.
I need Jesus in my life. Restore me, heal me and teach me*

to be more like You.
I receive Your Son Jesus as my personal Lord and Savior.
Amen!

I bless and congratulate you! Now, just believe in your heart that God has already forgiven you of all your sins, that you are a child of God right now, and that Jesus is Your Father, your Lord, and the King of all your life!

The next thing I would like to recommend is that you:

- Begin the process of spiritual growth and mature in your life as a believer of our Lord Jesus Christ and be guided by His Holy Spirit. **This process is known as discipleship.**

Remember that our mission is to preach the gospel to every creature and make disciples.

- A disciple is like a younger brother who is taught and helped by his older one to grow in the knowledge of God and His Word.

- To be a disciple is to have pastors, teachers, or mentors that shed light and revelation about those things that have not yet been revealed to you. Remember that it is very helpful to ask questions whenever in doubt. Do not be afraid to ask. After all, to learn is wise.

QUESTIONNAIRE

Exercise 1: Fill in the blank with the correct answer:

1. During Christmas, the world celebrates the _____ of Jesus, the Son of God.

2. During Holy Week, Christians celebrate the _____ and _____ of our savior.

3. According to John 3:16, "For God so loved the _____ that He gave His only begotten _____, that whoever believes in Him should not perish but have _____ life."

4. Complete the following portion of scripture from Philippians 2:7, "...but made Himself of no _____, taking the form of a _____."

5.

6. 5) Jesus was _____ of the virgin Mary. He was engendered by the _____.

7. Jesus laid down His life as a _____ without _____.

8. Christ paid the _____ for our sin by dying on the _____.

9. According to John 15:13, "Greater _____ has no one than this, than to lay down one's _____ for his friends."

10. Jesus came down to earth and _____ on the cross so that we might have life more _____.

11. Jesus came to give us _____ with an eternal purpose.

12. If you wish to have eternal life, you must receive Jesus Christ in your _____ and believe that He came and _____ on the cross for us.

13. He came to _____ us from sin.

14. Jesus came to _____ us from every vice and chain of bondage.

15. Jesus also delivers us from the second _____.

16. He wants to heal our bodies from every _____.

17. We now have the _____ through Jesus Christ our Lord!

3

The Holy Spirit

WHO IS THE HOLY SPIRIT?
LET'S TALK ABOUT HIM AS A PERSON
AND HIS WORK ON THE EARTH.

After Jesus rose again, He spent several weeks with His disciples, sharing with them. Shortly thereafter, a concern arose that they would be left alone, without the Presence of Jesus when He returned to the Father, for they were like a group of brothers and friends who went everywhere with Him.

And the master told them:

John 14:16
"And I will pray the Father, and He will give you another Helper, that He may abide with you forever."

And Jesus added:

John 14:26
"But the Helper, the Holy Spirit, whom the Father will send in My name, He will teach you all things, and bring to your remembrance all things that I said to you."

- This is the promise Jesus gave His disciples that they would receive: A Comforter.

- He further emphasized that they should wait for him together in the upper room.

- Around a hundred and twenty obeyed the Lord, persevering in unity and prayer. His other followers, however, were scattered.

Acts 1:8 shares a little more information on this event:
"But you shall receive power when the Holy Spirit has come upon you; and you shall be witnesses to Me in Jerusalem, and in all Judea and Samaria, and to the end of the earth."

There are three important things Jesus promises them:

- They will be filled with the Holy Spirit.

- They will receive power.

- They will be His witnesses on all the earth. That is, they will represent the life and witness of Jesus in ourselves.

And in **Acts 4:31** the promise is fulfilled:

"And when they had prayed, the place where they were assembled together was shaken; and they were all filled with the Holy Spirit, and they spoke the word of God with boldness."

- Those one hundred and twenty received the powerful infilling of the Holy Spirit and the commission to fulfill their calling. Now, they were ready to carry out their ministry and God-given assignment.

- Having received His gifts and power, the disciples were empowered by the infilling of the Holy Spirit to preach, disciple, and fulfill Jesus' Great Commission of going out and making disciples in all the world. They took the good news of salvation –the saving gospel of our Lord Jesus Christ– to every person and nation.

Let's recall, for a moment, the Great Commission found in **Matthew 28:19-20,**

19 "Go therefore and make disciples of all the nations, baptizing them in the name of the Father and of the Son and of the Holy Spirit,

20 teaching them to observe all things that I have commanded you; and lo, I am with you always, even to the end of the age. Amen."

- The Lord baptizes them with His Holy Spirit. The same thing happens to every believer when we receive Jesus Christ as our Lord and Savior.

- The process is complete once we enter the waters of baptism.

It is the beginning of our being equipped, enabled, and empowered by the Spirit of God. From then on, we continue being discipled and trained for the ministry God has prepared for every believer.

- Expanding on what the ministry is : It is the purpose or desire God places in every child's heart to do His work.

- God's purpose is eternal. We are to do it consistently as long as we are here on earth.

- The purpose of the ministry is to be sent out to help our neighbor, family, and anywhere He directs us.

- We are sent as the true beloved children of the living God, determined to be used by Him as children of light and Jesus' witnesses at all times and in all places.

- When God baptizes us with His Spirit, He fills us with His power.

- God fills us with the Holy Spirit and fire. Spiritually, this fire is known as the Dunamis of the Holy Spirit. You might be asking yourself what this is? It is a greater power, an anointing, an ability that manifests as signs, wonders, and miracles. It also allows us to speak in angelic tongues.

- The Holy Spirit fills us with God's precious presence, which manifests as a great and mighty anointing as we renew and cleanse our lives by obeying God's Word.

- The Holy Spirit's anointing also purifies our soul and mind from sinful thoughts.

- Little by little, as we are filled with His wonderful Presence, His glory is made manifest day-in and day-out in our lives. And we start being His witnesses wherever Jesus desires to use us with His great power.

NOW LET'S TALK A LITTLE ABOUT THE HOLY SPIRIT'S INCREDIBLE WORK.

The Holy Spirit's ministry has several goals in the life of every believer.

Jesus describes His purpose in **John 16:7-11**:

8 "Nevertheless I tell you the truth. It is to your advantage that I go away; for if I do not go away, the Helper will not come to you; but if I depart, I will send Him to you.

8 And when He has come, He will convict the world of sin, and of righteousness, and of judgment:

9 of sin, because they do not believe in Me;

10 of righteousness, because I go to My Father and you see Me no more;

11 of judgment, because the ruler of this world is judged."

In the church:

- **The Holy Spirit is the one who builds the church.**

Ephesians 2:19-22

19 "Now, therefore, you are no longer strangers and foreigners, but fellow citizens with the saints and

members of the household of God,
20 having been built on the foundation of the apostles and prophets, Jesus Christ Himself being the chief cornerstone,
21 in whom the whole building, being fitted together, grows into a holy temple in the Lord,
22 in whom you also are being built together for a dwelling place of God in the Spirit."

• **The Holy Spirit directs the missionary work:**

Acts 16:6 & 10
9 "Now when they had gone through Phrygia and the region of Galatia, they were forbidden by the Holy Spirit to preach the word in Asia."
10 "Now after he had seen the vision, immediately we sought to go to Macedonia, concluding that the Lord had called us to preach the gospel to them."

Acts 13: 2, 4
2 "As they ministered to the Lord and fasted, the Holy Spirit said, "Now separate to Me Barnabas and Saul for the work to which I have called them.
4 So, being sent out by the Holy Spirit, they went down to Seleucia, and from there they sailed to Cyprus."

• **The Holy Spirit chooses His workers:**

Acts 20:28
28 "Therefore take heed to yourselves and to all the flock, among which the Holy Spirit has made you overseers, to shepherd the church of God which He purchased with His own blood."

• **The Holy Spirit anoints His messengers:**

1 Corinthians 2:4

"And my speech and my preaching were not with persuasive words of human wisdom, but in demonstration of the Spirit and of power..."

- **The Holy Spirit is the one responsible for baptizing believers with power:**

Acts 2:1-4

1 "When the Day of Pentecost had fully come, they were all with one accord in one place.

2 And suddenly there came a sound from heaven, as of a rushing mighty wind, and it filled the whole house where they were sitting.

3 Then there appeared to them divided tongues, as of fire, and one sat upon each of them.

4 And they were all filled with the Holy Spirit and began to speak with other tongues, as the Spirit gave them utterance."

The Holy Spirit serves a very important purpose for all believers as a whole:

- **He Convicts us of sin.**

John 16:8

"And when He has come, He will convict the world of sin, and of righteousness, and of judgment:"

We could never be believers of the Gospel of our Lord Jesus Christ without his mighty intervention. This is one of his ministries as described in **John 16:8-11.**

- **Moreover, the Holy Spirit is responsible for regenerating and restoring us.**

Titus 3:5 says, "He has saved us, not by works of righteousness which we have done, but according to His mercy He saved us, through the washing of regeneration and renewing of the Holy Spirit..."

The Spirit is at work in us:

- He sanctifies us by taking a person's life and enabling them to live a life in righteousness and faith.

- The Holy Spirit dwells and lives within every believer.

1 Corinthians 3:16
"Do you not know that you are the temple of God and that the Spirit of God dwells in you?"

1 Corinthians 6:19-20
19 "Or do you not know that your body is the temple of the Holy Spirit who is in you, whom you have from God, and you are not your own?
20 For you were bought at a price; therefore, glorify God in your body and in your spirit, which are God's."

Additional references: **Galatians 5:16-18**

- **The Holy Spirit strengthens us.**

Ephesians 3:16
"that He would grant you, according to the riches of His glory, to be strengthened with might through His Spirit in the inner man."

- **The Holy Spirit intercedes for us before the Father.**

Romans 8:26

"Likewise, the Spirit also helps in our weaknesses. For we do not know what we should pray for as we ought, but the Spirit Himself makes intercession for us with groanings which cannot be uttered."

- **The Holy Spirit leads us.**

John 16:13

"However, when He, the Spirit of truth, has come, He will guide you into all truth; for He will not speak on His own authority, but whatever He hears He will speak; and He will tell you things to come."

- **The Holy Spirit shows us God's love.**

Romans 5:5

"Now hope does not disappoint, because the love of God has been poured out in our hearts by the Holy Spirit who was given to us."

- **The Holy Spirit fashions us into the image of Christ.**

2 Corinthians 3:18

"But we all, with unveiled face, beholding as in a mirror the glory of the Lord, are being transformed into the same image from glory to glory, just as by the Spirit of the Lord."

- **The Holy Spirit teaches us.**

1 John 2:27

"But the anointing which you have received from Him abides in you, and you do not need that anyone teach you; but as the same anointing teaches you concerning all things, and is true, and is not a lie, and just as it has taught you, you will abide in Him."

- **The Holy Spirit comforts us.**

2 Corinthians 1:4

"...who comforts us in all our tribulation, that we may be able to comfort those who are in any trouble, with the comfort with which we ourselves are comforted by God."

- **The Holy Spirit delivers us and gives us freedom.**

2 Corinthians 3:17

"Now the Lord is the Spirit; and where the Spirit of the Lord is, there is liberty."

- **The Holy Spirit gives us the assurance of our salvation.**

1 John 5:12

"He who has the Son has life; he who does not have the Son of God does not have life."

- **The Holy Spirit speaks through us.**

Mark 13:11

"But when they arrest you and deliver you up, do not worry beforehand, or premeditate what you will speak. But whatever is given you in that hour, speak that; for it is not you who speak, but the Holy Spirit."

- **The Holy Spirit revitalizes our bodies.**

Romans 8:11
"But if the Spirit of Him who raised Jesus from the dead dwells in you, He who raised Christ from the dead will also give life to your mortal bodies through His Spirit who dwells in you."

- **The Holy Spirit empowers us for the ministry by giving us gifts and growing His fruit in us.**

Ephesians 4:12
"...for the equipping of the saints for the work of ministry, for the edifying of the body of Christ."

- **The Holy Spirit has fellowship with us and reveals Christ to us.**

It is very difficult to have a relationship with Jesus without The Holy Spirit. That is why every child of God must be filled, baptized, and led by the person of the Holy Spirit.

God longs to bless us and transform our lives, but without the infilling of the Holy Spirit, there can be no radical changes or meaningful reformation in our lives.

God created and established us in His kingdom of light so that all his sons (children) would partake of His same holy nature, just as His son Jesus did.

Genesis 1:2
"The earth was without form, and void; and darkness was on the face of the deep. And the Spirit of God was hovering over the face of the waters."

We can see how the Holy Spirit was present in the world's creation. Just like Jesus, he was also together with the Father, creating the universe and all things visible and invisible.

This passage clearly says that the Spirit moved upon the waters. And the word move means: action, to move, to change, to sway, to displace, to transfer. It means that the Holy Spirit hovered over the waters. He was active in creation. He had an active role in the creative process, forming everything at the beginning of all things.

Applying this to our life, we should earnestly desire the Holy Spirit to move in our entire spirit and soul. We must allow Him to take the necessary steps and bring about a transformation in our inner man, fully guided and directed by God.

In other words, we must ask the Holy Spirit to transfer us from the kingdom of darkness to the kingdom of light, to the light of the first day, the true light that emanates from the very presence of the Father of lights.

On that first day of creation, God said, "Let there be light, and there was light". **Genesis 1:3-5**

- However, we lost that light when Adam and Eve sinned. But, as we are reconciled to Christ, we recover it again and become part of the light of the first day.

- With the Holy Spirit, our sin consciousness is removed and revealed to us. And we begin to desire to identify any sin that might manifest in our mind and The Holy Spirit reveals and removes our sin consciousness within us. And we start to identify any sin that might manifest in our minds and heart.

- When we consciously have the Holy Spirit operating in us, we can immediately free ourselves from every sinful thought by confessing our sin to Him and repenting.

We should all strive to be continually filled with His wonderful Holy Spirit to become victorious believers who overcome and reach the stature of the perfect man, Jesus Christ.

How many are starting to feel encouraged to remain in Him?

- If we are not encouraged to live in the Spirit, we'll have to settle for a life void of victories, filled with griping and complaining —a life lacking maturity or spiritual growth. We will spend our days and even years idly sitting in a chair every time we go to church.

- Without the Holy Spirit, we will only engage in a Christian religion but not a communion-fille relationship with the Spirit of God Himself.

If we are not activated in our spirit, our spiritual waters will remain stagnant, becoming a lifeless well with no currents or movement. No one desires to live this way. We were created to be constantly moving, producing glorious lives, just like our Lord Jesus Christ.

He longs to see every believer filled with the waters of His Holy Spirit and have those rivers of living water flow throughout our entire being!

Our Lord longs to see the ripening of every one of the Holy Spirit's delectable fruits growing and manifesting in our lives every day.

To conclude this wonderful subject of the Holy Spirit, we want to state that we have one God who manifests Himself in three divine persons: the Father, Jesus the Son, and the Holy Spirit −all as one God.

- **The Holy Spirit is the power and presence of God in us.**

He is the part that allows us to see and experience God. And that is why we so need him in our lives.

We must strive to seek God, long for Him, cherish Him, and never grieve, blaspheme, or speak against Him.

It is He who enables, empowers, and gives us the gifts to carry out His work and our prophetic destiny.

- **The Holy Spirit gives us presents, spiritual gifts. We can learn more about them in 1 Corinthians 12:1-11.**

The fruit of the Spirit manifests as love, faith, patience, self-control, wisdom, word of knowledge, healings, miracles, and gifts of prophecy. In other individuals, He manifests as the discernment of spirits, the gift of tongues, and the gift of interpretation of tongues.

Every gift is a part of the person of God, which He bestows on us so we may walk as Jesus walked.

That is why it is so essential to remain continually revived by the Holy Spirit!

1 Thessalonians 5:19 exhorts us to, *"never quench the Holy Spirit."*

Ephesians 4:30-32 also cautions us,
30 And do not grieve the Holy Spirit of God, by whom you were sealed for the day of redemption.
31 Let all bitterness, wrath, anger, clamor, and evil speaking be put away from you, with all malice.
32 And be kind to one another, tenderhearted, forgiving one another, even as God in Christ forgave you."
Amen!

QUESTIONNAIRE

Exercise 1: Fill in the blank with the correct answer.

1.   What did Jesus ask for in John 14:16?

"And I will _____ the Father, and He will give you another _____, that He may abide with you forever."

2. According to John 14:26, what two things will the Holy Spirit do for us?

a)_____

b)_____

3. Where did the disciples receive the infilling of the Holy Spirit? They were in the _____? How many were filled? _____.

4. In which book of the Bible do we find this event?

_____

5. According to Acts 1:8, what did the disciples receive with the outpouring of the Holy Spirit? They received _____ to be His _____.

Exercise 2: Reviewing the works of the Holy Spirit, write the correct Bible verse from the box on each line:

1) Perfects the saints and builds the body of Christ (church): _____

2) Speaks to us and guides us:_____

3) Intercedes for us:_____

4) Comforts us:_____

5) Teaches us:_____

6) Fills us with His Power:_____

7) Gives us assurance that we have life in the Son:_____

8) Shows us God's love:_____

9) Convicts us of sin: _____

10) Frees and delivers us:_____

11) Speaks through us: _____

12) Quickens our bodies: _____

13) Gives us spiritual gifts: _____

Bible verse:

2 Corinthians 3:17 - 1 John 2:27 - Mark 13:11

Ephesians 4:12-15 - 2 Corinthians 1:4 - John 16:8

John 16:13 - Romans 5:5ç -   Romans 8:26

1 Corinthians 12:1-12 - 1 John 5:12 - Romans 8:11

Acts 1:8

4

Water Baptism

B aptism is a Greek word that means "to immerse in water".

To be immersed in water through baptism is to submerge in the body and life of Christ and take on the identity as a true child of the living God.

- **Baptism is a command from Jesus.**

Matthew 28:19-20
19 Go therefore and make disciples of all the nations baptizing them in the name of the Father and of the Son and of the Holy Spirit,
20 teaching them to observe all things that I have commanded you; and lo, I am with you always, even to the end of the age." Amen.

John's baptism is unto repentance, but the baptism in the Holy Spirit is somewhat different, and I will explain it.

We should seek to be baptized not only in water but also in the Holy Spirit. In addition to baptism being a testimony, we are also given the opportunity to be baptized in fire and filled with the power of God with signs and manifestations, such as speaking in other tongues. These demonstrations sound powerful, don't they?

LET'S LEARN A LITTLE MORE ABOUT WATER BAPTISM

Acts 18:24-26

24 "Now a certain Jew named Apollos, born at Alexandria, an eloquent man and mighty in the Scriptures, came to Ephesus.
25 This man had been instructed in the way of the Lord; and being fervent in spirit, he spoke and taught accurately the things of the Lord, though he knew only the baptism of John.
26 So he began to speak boldly in the synagogue. When Aquila and Priscilla heard him, they took him aside and explained to him the way of God more accurately."

Acts 19:1-7

1 And it happened, while Apollos was at Corinth, that Paul, having passed through the upper regions, came to Ephesus. And finding some disciples
2 he said to them, "Did you receive the Holy Spirit when

you believed?" So they said to him, "We have not so much as heard whether there is a Holy Spirit."

3 And he said to them, "Into what then were you baptized?" So they said, "Into John's baptism."

4 Then Paul said, "John indeed baptized with a baptism of repentance, saying to the people that they should believe on Him who would come after him, that is, on Christ Jesus."

5 When they heard this, they were baptized in the name of the Lord Jesus.

6 And when Paul had laid hands on them, the Holy Spirit came upon them, and they spoke with tongues and prophesied.

7 Now the men were about twelve in all."

- Baptism is a public witness to let others know that we have received Jesus Christ as the Lord of our life.

- Spiritually, water baptism symbolizes the death and burial of Jesus and the resurrection to new life in Him.

It is a powerful experience! We should desire to be baptized in water.

Mark 16:16

"He who believes and is baptized will be saved; but he who does not believe will be condemned."

- The only requirement to be baptized is to believe that Jesus Christ is the Son of God and accept that He died to forgive our sins.

BORN OF THE WATER AND THE SPIRIT

John 3:5

"Jesus answered, 'Most assuredly, I say to you unless one is born of water and the Spirit, he cannot enter the kingdom of God.'"

- To be born of the water means to be born of Christ because Jesus is the living water. It means to be immersed in His waters.

- To be born of the Spirit means to be baptized in the Holy Spirit and be led by His voice.

After we start to know Him and His Word and begin to be formed and discipled in Him, God commands us to share His great love and sacrifice with others so that they, too, might be saved.

Matthew 28:19-20

19" Go therefore and make disciples of all the nations, baptizing them in the name of the Father and of the Son and of the Holy Spirit,
20 teaching them to observe all things that I have commanded you; and lo, I am with you always even to the end of the age." Amen.

UNDERSTANDING MORE ABOUT BAPTISM ACCORDING TO SCRIPTURE

1 Peter 3:21

"There is also an antitype which now saves us— baptism (not the removal of the filth of the flesh, but the

answer of a good conscience toward God), through the resurrection of Jesus Christ..."

Acts 2:38

"Then Peter said to them, "Repent, and let every one of you be baptized in the name of Jesus Christ for the remission of sins; and you shall receive the gift of the Holy Spirit."

Acts 9:12

"And in a vision, he has seen a man named Ananias coming in and putting his hand on him, so that he might receive his sight."

Acts 22:15-16

15 "For you will be His witness to all men of what you have seen and heard.
16 And now why are you waiting? Arise and be baptized, and wash away your sins, calling on the name of the Lord."

1 Corinthians 2:13

"These things we also speak, not in words which man's wisdom teaches but which the Holy Spirit teaches, comparing spiritual things with spiritual."

Acts 2:41

"Then those who gladly received his word were baptized; and that day about three thousand souls were added to them."

WHY ARE WE BAPTIZED?

- We are baptized because it is a commandment of Jesus Christ.

- Also, because once saved, we are baptized by the Holy Spirit into the body of Christ, which is the church, and are grafted into the family of God.

1 Corinthians 12:13
"For by one Spirit we were all baptized into one body—whether Jews or Greeks, whether slaves or free—and have all been made to drink [a]into one Spirit."

- Water baptism is the ceremony or act of the baptism in the Holy Spirit.

- Water baptism is a public proclamation of our faith. Through this act, we proclaim that we have truly surrendered our life, soul, and spirit to God to obey and believe in His Word and His promises.

- Baptism is the starting point of discipleship, to be trained to fulfill our calling and purpose in this life.

- Baptism represents a believer's identification with the death, burial, and resurrection of Christ.

Every person who comes to their faith in Christ must be baptized. By doing so, they bear witness to being believers in the Lord Jesus Christ, who dwells in their hearts.

Colossians 2:12

"...buried with Him in baptism, in which you also were raised with Him through faith in the working of God, who raised Him from the dead."

Romans 6:4

"Therefore, we were buried with Him through baptism into death, that just as Christ was raised from the dead by the glory of the Father, even so we also should walk in newness of life."

- The Bible points out that baptism is required to be saved.

- Following salvation, Christian baptism is an act of obedience to the Lord Jesus Christ.

The Scriptures shows us various places and examples where people repented of their sin and were immediately baptized.

Acts 2:41

"Then those who gladly received his word were baptized; and that day about three thousand souls were added to them."

Acts 16:14-15

14 "Now a certain woman named Lydia heard us. She was a seller of purple from the city of Thyatira, who worshiped God. The Lord opened her heart to heed the things spoken by Paul.
15 And when she and her household were baptized, she begged us, saying, 'If you have judged me to be faithful to the Lord, come to my house and stay.' So, she persuaded us."

In addition, we will also see what happened in the case of Philip and the eunuch in **Acts 8:35-36**,

35 "Then Philip opened his mouth, and beginning at this Scripture, preached Jesus to him.
36 Now as they went down the road, they came to some water. And the eunuch said, 'See, here water. What hinders me from being baptized?'"

CUESTIONARIO

Exercise 1: Fill in the blanks with the correct word or phrase from the box:

Repentance - baptized - immersed in water Matthew 28:19-20 - immersed in Christ - filled with power public witness - John 3:15 - Christ cannot enter the Kingdom of God

1. The Greek word for "baptism" means to be :_____.

2. Baptism is commanded in the Bible in the following scripture:_____.

3. To be baptized means to be: _____-

4. When you are baptized with the Holy Spirit, you are:_____.

5. The Baptism of John was unto:_____

6. When you are baptized you become a:_____.

7. The following scripture is found in:_____ "... that whosoever believes in Him should not perish but have everlasting life."

8. To be born of the water means to be born of:_____

9. "All those who believe and are _____ shall be saved."

10. Those who are not born of the water and the Spirit _____.

5

The Lord's Supper

YOU HAVE PROBABLY ASKED YOURSELF MANY TIMES, WHAT IS THE LORD'S SUPPER?

The answer is clearly stated in the following Bible scripture.

Luke 22:19-20

19 And He took bread, gave thanks and broke it, and gave it to them, saying, "This is My body which is given for you; do this in remembrance of Me."
20 Likewise He also took the cup after supper saying, "This cup is the new covenant in My blood, which is shed for you."

- Jesus Himself instituted the Lord's Supper.

- The text says that Jesus "took the bread, broke it,

and gave thanks." The bread symbolizes His body and flesh, which was given for us all.

His body was bruised, wounded, broken, lacerated, beaten, and offered as a living sacrifice for all humankind.

- The verses also stipulate that every time we choose to partake of the Lord's Supper (communion,) we do so in remembrance of Him.

By taking communion, we remember Jesus' sacrifice and appreciate His death on the cross of Calvary.

- When Jesus took the cup of grape juice or wine, He said, "This cup is the new covenant in my blood which is poured out for you."

The blood of Jesus Christ is pictured with grape wine. By drinking it, we drink His mighty blood, and by eating the bread, we partake of His flesh.

- The life of Jesus Christ is represented in the flesh and blood, and by ingesting them, we make them life with our own body.

His blood becomes one with mine. His flesh becomes one body with mine. His life quickens my own, and the power of His resurrection causes me to rise with Jesus and be one in Him —one body and one Spirit— establishing His mind, holiness, and wholeness in my entire being.

It is so glorious to partake of the Lord's Supper as often as we want to! It is a wonderful privilege as long as we recognize the exceedingly great value of His death and resurrection and that we also live in complete holiness.

Of course, it also means doing it in complete faith!

1 Corinthians 10:16-17

16 "The cup of blessing which we bless, is it not the communion of the blood of Christ? The bread which we break, is it not the communion of the body of Christ?
17 For we, though many, are one bread and one body; for we all partake of that one bread."

1 Corinthians 11:26

"For as often as you eat this bread and drink this cup, you proclaim the Lord's death till He comes."

THE INSTITUTION OF THE LORD'S SUPPER

We find it in the following verses:

Mark 13:23-25 and Luke 22:14-20.

23 For I received from the Lord that which I also delivered to you: that the Lord Jesus on the same night in which He was betrayed took bread;
24 and when He had given thanks, He broke it and said, "Take, eat; this is My body which is broken for you; do this in remembrance of Me."
25 In the same manner He also took the cup after supper, saying, "This cup is the new covenant in My blood. This do as often as you drink it, in remembrance of Me."

Matthew 26:26-28

26 "And as they were eating, Jesus took bread, blessed and broke it, and gave it to the disciples and said, 'Take,

eat; this is My body.'
27 Then He took the cup, and gave thanks, and gave it to them, saying, 'Drink from it, all of you.
28 For this is My blood of the new covenant, which is shed for many for the remission of sins.'"

WHEN SHOULD WE CELEBRATE THE LORD'S SUPPER?

- To celebrate the resurrection.
- To acknowledge that Christ died on the cross and shed His precious blood for all mankind.
- For deliverance, restoration and healing.

There is power when we celebrate Holy Communion!

John 6:53
"Then Jesus said to them, 'Most assuredly, I say to you, unless you eat the flesh of the Son of Man and drink His blood, you have no life in you.'"

- It means that if we take Jesus' words literally, we should frequently take communion and be filled with the life of Christ so that healing, deliverance, and blessings will abound.

John 6:56-58
56 "He who eats My flesh and drinks My blood abides in Me, and I in him.

Jesus, Himself talks to us about abiding in Him, always living to please Him, dwelling in His presence, and immersing in Him and His living waters.

57 As the living Father sent Me, and I live because of the Father, so he who feeds on Me will live because of Me. 58 This is the bread which came down from heaven, not as your fathers ate the manna, and are dead. He who eats this bread will live forever."

In the Lord's Supper, the bread is not just a symbol of his body.

But Christ's body is "true food" and his blood, "true drink."

And he who eats His body and drinks His blood shall live and have eternal life.

Let's look back at **Matthew 26:28** for a moment:
"For this is My blood of the new covenant, which is shed for many for the remission of sins."

- His blood of the New Covenant is for the forgiveness of sins.

Redemption means that the blood of Jesus Christ has already redeemed our sins. In other words, we have already been forgiven!

Mark 14:22
"And as they were eating, Jesus took bread, blessed and broke it, and gave it to them and said, "Take, eat; this is My body."

Notice that Jesus' expression in this verse is in the present tense, therefore it cannot be a symbol.

- The bread is the body of Christ. And the grape wine is the blood He shed for the forgiveness of our sins.

Hebrews 8:22
"And according to the law almost all things are purified with blood, and without shedding of blood there is no remission."

1 Corinthians 11:25 answers the question as to how often we should celebrate AND participate in the Lord's Supper:
"In the same manner He also took the cup after supper, saying, 'This cup is the new covenant in My blood. This do as often as you drink it, in remembrance of Me.'"

- We can take communion as often as possible, as long as we always do so in remembrance of the blood that He shed in His sacrifice.

The formats and requirements for the Lord's Supper are set forth in His Word:

1 Corinthians 5:7-8
7 Therefore purge out the old leaven, that you may be a new lump, since you truly are unleavened. For indeed Christ, our Passover, was sacrificed for us.
8 Therefore let us keep the feast, not with old leaven, nor with the leaven of malice and wickedness, but with the unleavened bread of sincerity and truth.

1 Corinthians 11:28
"But let a man examine himself, and so let him eat of the bread and drink of the cup."

It is quite clear that before partaking of the Lord's Supper, we must be cleansed from the old leaven. What does this mean??

- The old leaven represents sin, wickedness, rebellion, and iniquity.

- We must repent of every sin in our lives before we eat and drink of Him.

Why must we be cleansed?

- The Word of God says that by taking communion in an 'unworthy manner,' we can bring curses and even sickness into our lives.

A BRIEF HISTORICAL OVERVIEW

The Lord's Supper in the Old Testament.

Genesis 14:17-21

17 "And the king of Sodom went out to meet him at the Valley of Shaveh (that is, the King's Valley), after his return from the defeat of Chedorlaomer and the kings who were with him.
18 Then Melchizedek king of Salem brought out bread and wine; he was the priest of God Most High.
19 And he blessed him and said: "Blessed be Abram of God Most High, Possessor of heaven and earth;
20 And blessed be God Most High, who has delivered your enemies into your hand." And he gave him a tithe of all.
21 Now the king of Sodom said to Abram, "Give me the persons, and take the goods for yourself."

According to **Hebrews 7:2-3**, Melchizedek is, *"to whom also Abraham gave a tenth part of all, first being translated "king of righteousness," and then also king of Salem, meaning "king of peace," without father, without mother, without genealogy, having neither beginning of days nor end of life, but made like the Son of God, remains a priest continually."*

Moreover, He blessed Abraham after sharing the bread and the wine.

Looking back at the book of **Isaiah 53:3-5**, it says:
3 "He is despised and rejected by men, a Man of sorrows and acquainted with grief. And we hid, as it were, our faces from Him; He was despised, and we did not esteem Him.
4 Surely, He has borne our griefs and carried our sorrows; yet we esteemed Him stricken, smitten by God, and afflicted.
5 But He was wounded for our transgressions. He was bruised for our iniquities; the chastisement for our peace was upon Him, and by His stripes we are healed."

- When we speak of the Lord's Supper, we commemorate the vicarious sacrifice Jesus made in our place.

By shedding his blood for our salvation and being wounded for our healing, the Lamb of God has become our eternal and great high priest.

Note: If a person partaking of the Lord's Supper has any unconfessed iniquities, he does so in an unworthy manner.

1 Corinthians 11:27-34

27 "Therefore whoever eats this bread or drinks this cup of the Lord in an unworthy manner will be guilty of the body and blood of the Lord.

28 But let a man examine himself, and so let him eat of the bread and drink of the cup.

29 For he who eats and drinks in an unworthy manner eats and drinks judgment to himself, not discerning the Lord's body.

30 For this reason many are weak and sick among you, and many sleep.

31 For if we would judge ourselves, we would not be judged.

32 But when we are judged, we are chastened by the Lord, that we may not be condemned with the world.

33 Therefore, my brethren, when you come together to eat, wait for one another.

34 But if anyone is hungry, let him eat at home, lest you come together for judgment. And the rest I will set in order when I come."

The consequences of taking communion in an unworthy manner, without honoring the body of Christ or discerning that it really is the Lord's body, are quite grave, indeed.

- Verse 34 above shows us that such an individual:
  "...will be guilty of the body and blood of the Lord," sinning against the body and blood of Christ by not acknowledging Him as their Savior and repenting of their sins.

- Verses 29 and 30 are clear about this: "...eats and drinks judgment to himself, not discerning the Lord's body. For this reason, many are weak and sick among you, and many sleep."

It is the reason why many of our brethren are sick and weak to resist sin, quickly succumbing to temptation, while others have grown cold, spiritually dead.

- "But when we are judged, we are chastened by the Lord." For this offense, the Lord chastises us to learn and not be condemned by those in the world.

To avoid these tragic consequences, we are urged to eat the Lord's Supper "worthily." The same portion of scripture gives us the following recommendations:

- "But let every person examine themselves, and so let them eat..." Everyone must examine his own conscience before eating of the bread and drinking of the cup.

- "...discern the body of the Lord," means to realize that it is the body of Christ and partake of it with an attitude of reverence and gratitude for His great sacrifice.

- To examine ourselves means to check ourselves inwardly.

- And once we are convicted of sin, repent intimately, within our soul and spirit, so that the Lord will not have to punish us so long as "....that we may not be condemned with the world."

If we don't examine ourselves then who will?

The passage of scriptures offers one final recommendation:

- To wait for one another to eat.

It is about showing love and an attitude of respect and consideration for our brethren. This warning is designed to prevent our celebrations of the Lord's Supper from provoking judgment rather than a blessing.

I want to remind you that there are many benefits to taking Communion in a worthy manner.

It is critically important to understand that it's the attitude with which we partake of the Lord's Supper that activates the blessings in our lives:

- Being thankful for the bread and the wine.

- Remembering that our Lord Jesus Christ's DNA is in the wine.

- Believing by faith that if we have any sickness in our body, the blood of Christ becomes one with our blood, bringing healing, and that his flesh becomes one with ours.

WHAT TAKES PLACE IN OUR SOUL AND OUR SPIRIT WHEN WE PARTAKE OF THE LORD'S SUPPER?

- Once the blood of Christ unites with our spirit, it heals our blood and our body.

- In addition, it also cleanses our minds and hearts and our spiritual DNA.

- The blood of Jesus cleanses all of our organs. Through it, we declare wholeness in every one of our cells and every chromosome within them is healed in Jesus' name.

Our minds and thoughts are restored when we receive His mighty blood in us.

LET'S PRAY

Father, thank You!
Because Your blood wipes away every wound from my heart.
My soul is healed of all rejection, torment, and sickness in Jesus' name.
We declare freedom from every doubt. Every darkness in my mind must now leave.
I rise up and come out of every dark place, out into the light, to dwell in heavenly and peaceful places.
In Jesus' name, let Your blood and mine come together to form a glorious fortress.
Amen!
My body is whole. Thank You, Father!
Thank You, Jesus, for Your blood and Your flesh. In Your mighty name we pray,
Amen!

QUESTIONNAIRE

Exercise 1: Fill in the blank with the correct answer.

1) According to Luke 22:19-20, "And He took the _____, gave thanks and broke it, and gave it to them, saying, "This is My _____ which is given for you; do this in remembrance of Me." Likewise He also took the _____ after supper, saying, "This cup is the new _____ __ in My blood, which is shed for you.

2) 1 Corinthians 11:26 says, "For as often as you eat this bread and _____ this cup, you _____ the Lord's _____ till He comes."

3) How often can we celebrate the Lord's Supper?

_____

4) According to John 6:53, 56-58, which element represents the body of Jesus Christ? _____
Which element represents His blood? _____

5) According to 1 Corinthians 11:28 what is the main requirement to take communion?

_____

6) Name 3 negative outcomes from partaking of the Lord's Supper in an unworthy manner according to 1 Corinthians 11:30...

a)_____   b)_____
c)_____

7) Mention 2 main blessings we receive when we take communion:

a)_____   b)_____

6

Repentance

WHAT DOES IT MEAN TO REPENT?

To repent is to confess your sins to God the Father. It means making a 180° turn in your life, changing bad habits, behaviors, and traditions that are outside of the Father's will.

It involves no longer doing what is wrong or contrary to God's will and ceasing from doing all that is against God's law and His commandments.

Furthermore, to repent means to stop doing anything against the law governing the nation where we live.
Have you ever wondered what it's like to repent from the heart?

I will show you how to do it, and by the end of the chapter, you will know how to say a prayer of repentance.

In the meanwhile, let's take a look at some verses from the Word of God (The Bible) that are easy to understand.

Romans 10:9

"...that if you confess with your mouth the Lord Jesus and believe in your heart that God has raised Him from the dead, you will be saved."

- The emphasis on confession here is found in:
  Declaring it with your mouth and believing it in your heart.

Romans 10:13 further explains:

"...for whoever calls on the name of the Lord shall be saved."

- To 'call on' means to cry out, to call on God by His name, for example, by saying, "Jesus, you are my Savior and my Lord."

- Confession of our sins:
  We understand that by confessing and believing wholeheartedly in Jesus as Lord, we also believe He died for all our sins and those of all humankind. Thus, we must utter a confession. We must ask our Heavenly Father, the God of all Creation, to forgive us for all our sins.

- Confession means recognizing that we are a sinner:
  It means to truly be mindful that we have failed God.

- Moreover, confession also means being aware that we need His forgiveness, love, and mercy.

1 John 1:9 says,

"If we confess our sins, He is faithful and just to forgive us our sins and to cleanse us from all unrighteousness."

- We must openly confess and tell God all our sins, both past and present.

For example, a heartfelt confession might sound something like the following:

Lord, I have lied so many times; I recognize that I have made lying a natural part of my life.
Besides, I have always liked to take what belongs to others without asking for it first.
Father, I also tend to think negatively of all my friends.
But today, Heavenly Father, I recognize that all these things were wrong, and You don't like them. It doesn't give me any peace of mind, either.
Today, I repent of all these sins with all my heart. Please, forgive me, Lord.
In Jesus' precious name I pray, amen!

Romans 5:8
"But God demonstrates His own love toward us, in that while we were still sinners, Christ died for us."

However, we also need to face this other truth.

Romans 3:23,
"...for all have sinned and come short of the Glory of God..."

When it says that we have all come short, that includes me; and not only me but every other human being on Earth as well.

- To repent also means to humble ourselves before God.

2 Chronicles 7:14

"If My people who are called by My name will humble themselves, and pray and seek My face, and turn from their wicked ways, then I will hear from heaven, and will forgive their sin and heal their land."

God commands us to humble our hearts, leave all pride aside, and come before Him. In exchange, He promises to hear our needs and desires from Heaven.

- As we repent, God will forgive us. He will restore us from our wrongful way of living.

He also makes us a new creation, a new and better person with greater wisdom and intelligence. As if that weren't enough, He also increases the faith in our hearts.

Did you know that the very moment you choose to repent, wonderful things happen in Heaven? Yes, you'll see!

Let's take a look at **Luke 15:7**

"I say to you that likewise there will be more joy in heaven over one sinner who repents than over ninety-nine just persons who need no repentance."

It says here that a celebration takes place in Heaven! That they celebrate our decision to become a child of God. Amen! This is real!

- In Heaven, there is joy, and together with the angels, Jesus celebrates our decision to be His child and be in Him.

Proverbs 28:13
"He who covers his sins will not prosper, but
whoever confesses and forsakes them will have mercy."

It means that for us to live prosperous lives, we must confess every sin and iniquity that we have inherited and has plagued us for many generations.

Among these inherited curses, for example, we have sickness, poverty, lack, vices, and many more.

All these curses are a product of not asking God's forgiveness for our past iniquities and present sins.

- Iniquity is the inheritance we all carry that causes us to fall into terrible sins.

It is a subject that we will expand on later in the following levels of discipleship.

In the meantime, here are some additional scriptures we can read about concerning repentance:

Romans 6:13
"And do not present your members as instruments of
unrighteousness to sin but present yourselves to God
as being alive from the dead, and your members as
instruments of righteousness to God."

Ezekiel 18:30b
"Repent, and turn from all your transgressions, so that
iniquity will not be your ruin."

Isaiah 1:16
"Wash yourselves, make yourselves clean; Put away the

evil of your doings from before My eyes. Cease to do evil..."

Psalms 32:5

"I acknowledged my sin to You, and my iniquity I have not hidden. I said, 'I will confess my transgressions to the Lord,' and You forgave the iniquity of my sin. Selah"

Daniel 9:5

"We have sinned and committed iniquity, we have done wickedly and rebelled, even by departing from Your precepts and Your judgments."

Titus 2:14

"...who gave Himself for us, that He might redeem us from every lawless deed and purify for Himself His own special people, zealous for good works."

Isaiah 53:5

"But He was wounded for our transgressions. He was bruised for our iniquities; the chastisement for our peace was upon Him, and by His stripes we are healed."

Now, as we learn about these promises of God, why not pray with me and ask God for forgiveness, repent of every sin, and confess Jesus Christ as your Lord and Savior?

PRAYER OF REPENTANCE

Let's pray:

Blessed Heavenly Father,
I know that I am a sinner and that it separates me from

You.
I come to you today, Father, and I repent of all my sins.
I place them on the cross, where I recognize that Jesus
gave His life for me. I lay them at the feet of Christ, and
I understand that by His precious blood, He cleanses and
forgives me.
And He also writes my name in the book of life.
Dear Father, please deliver me from every iniquity,
unrighteousness and bondage.
Bring me out of captivity and heal every sickness in my
body.
Today I declare myself a child of God, of the living God,
of the God who loves me.
Today, I am completely free to love You and be Your
beloved child.
I receive You into my heart Jesus.
Come into my life and take full control.
Make me a new person.
I love You.
In your name we pray, Amen.
Thank you, Lord!
Thank you, Father!

Praise God for saying this powerful prayer! I know God has heard you because His word says that He hears the prayer of every sinner who repents.

John 9:31 says, *"Now we know that God does not hear sinners; but if anyone is a worshiper of God and does His will, He hears him."*

- Moreover, the Scriptures say that the first prayer our Heavenly Father hears is the prayer of repentance which saves our soul.

This powerful prayer is the key to entering His Presence and presenting our hearts and all our requests to Him.

Prayer is our divine connection to His throne of grace.

Here's an example of how this works:

When you sign a contract for a new phone line with a communications company, they usually send a technician to your home who says, "All ready!" once the installation is done. You can now use your new phone and make calls.

You then dial the number you want to call to confirm it works and that others can listen and answer you. And you feel so happy!

Well, the same thing happens with this verse in **John 9:31**.

We must have faith in God, because salvation only works by faith, through grace.

Ephesians 2:8-9
> 8 *"For by grace you have been saved through faith, and that not of yourselves; it is the gift of God,*
> *9 not of works, lest anyone should boast."*

- God's grace is unmerited favor. Our Heavenly Father's mercy and love are free for all mankind through Jesus Christ.

Ephesians 2:10
> *"For we are His workmanship, created in Christ Jesus for good works, which God prepared beforehand that we should walk in them."*

Let me share a personal note. I am a fashion designer by profession. I make original and exclusive designs for each of my clients. I can create and make something totally original out of nothing.

We can compare this analogy to the apostle Paul when he said, "We are his workmanship." We were created in Christ to do good works.

Our original purpose is to carry out the designs the Father prepared and created beforehand for every one of his children.

Before ever even forming us, God designed a work for each of His children to perform. It is our responsibility to discover and carry out that purpose for which we have been assigned.

I invite you to a word of prayer as we recognize that we are saved solely by our Heavenly Father's grace and great love.

PRAYER

Heavenly Father,
Today, I understand that I am saved by Your grace and mercy.
Thank you for thinking of me and designing a destiny and a purpose for me, and for making me in your image and likeness, in Jesus' Name, amen!

QUESTIONNAIRE

Exercise 1: Fill in the blank with the correct answer:

1. The word that describes when we confess our sins to the Lord is:_____.

2. According to Romans 10:9 I must confess the Lord Jesus with my _____ and believe in my _____ that God has raised Him from the dead.

3. Everyone who calls on the Name of the _____, shall be saved.

4. It is my _____ that separate me from God.

5. We must confess our sins to God because we need His _____.

6. According to John 1:9, "God is _____ and just to _____ us our sins and cleanse us from all unrighteousness."

7. What happens in Heaven every time a sinner comes to repentance?_____

8. Proverbs 28:13 says, "He who covers his _____ will not prosper, but whoever _____ and _____ them will have mercy.

9. How long will Jesus be my savior?_____

10. After I confess my sins, God is faithful to _____ them.

7

Forgiveness

Learning to feel forgiven by our Father is very important after repenting of our sins.

- God's forgiveness is His manifest love through the precious blood of our Lord Jesus Christ. It's this forgiveness that washes us clean and cleanses us from all our rebellion and disobedience.

Once God forgives us, we are as white as snow and wool. Notice what David the psalmist says concerning this:

Psalms 51:7 y 10
7 *"Purge me with hyssop, and I shall be clean; wash me, and I shall be whiter than snow.*
10 *"Create in me a clean heart, O God, and renew a steadfast spirit within me."*

- Knowing we are forgiven makes us a people that is both healthy and redeemed.

To forgive means:

- To pay a debt. The bill is paid in full.
- God forgives every person who seeks Him and humbles themselves before Him. He does so as an act of love, mercy, and grace.
- Then, as we forgive others, we also emulate God. It is a reciprocal deed that every believer must practice.

Matthew 6:14-15 says, *"For if you forgive men their trespasses, your heavenly Father will also forgive you. But if you do not forgive men their trespasses, neither will your Father forgive your trespasses."*

- We must forgive everyone's offenses, no matter how great they are just, as God has promised to forgive ours as well.

Mark 11:25 says, *"And whenever you stand praying, if you have anything against anyone, forgive him, that your Father in heaven may also forgive you your trespasses."*

- Bear in mind that the Bible also says that there is no one who has never sinned. Hence, we all need forgiveness.

John 1:18 exhorts us,
"If we say that we have no sin, we deceive ourselves, and the truth is not in us."

That is why we must confess our sins every time we realize we have committed them.

There is a wonderful promise for us in 1 **John 1:9,** *"If we confess our sins, He is faithful and just to forgive us our sins and to cleanse us from all unrighteousness."*

Thus, we can rest assured that no matter how great or small the fault might be, once we confess our sins and the evil or iniquity that produces them, God will cleanse them from our hearts.

- By forgiving and being forgiven as children of God, we not only feel liberated and free of all guilt, but He also fills us with overwhelming joy.

David the psalmist said: *"Blessed (fortunate) is he whose transgression is forgiven, whose sin is covered."*- **Psalms 32:1**

The Bible also shes light on just how often we must be willing to forgive others —even our enemies.

On one occasion, the disciples were talking about this subject with Jesus, and we find their conversation in **Matthew 18:21-22,**
"Then Peter came to Him and said, "Lord, how often shall my brother sin against me, and I forgive him? Up to seven times?" Jesus said to him, "I do not say to you, up to seven times, but up to seventy times seven."

- By forgiving, we free our brothers and debtors from the tormentors (demons) who continually torment them with guilt and accusation.

- Forgiveness is one of the fruits of true repentance. It is an act of acknowledging our sins and faults as we turn to the Father in complete humility for salvation and reconciliation.

In addition to the above, there are many other benefits to forgiveness:

Acts 2:38 says, *"Then Peter said to them, 'Repent, and let every one of you be baptized in the name of Jesus Christ for the remission of sins; and you shall receive the gift of the Holy Spirit.'"*

- Receiving the baptism and infilling of His mighty Holy Spirit is one of the greatest privileges and blessings we can receive when we repent, forgive, and are forgiven by God.

We do all this by faith, believing our Heavenly Father at His Word.

QUESTIONNAIRE

Exercise 1: Fill in the blank with the correct answer.

1. Once God forgives our sins we are as white as:_____.

2. Psalms 51:8 says, "Create in me a clean _____, O God, and renew a right _____ within me."

3. To forgive means that the debt is paid in_____.

4. John 1:8 says, ""If we say that we have no sin we _____ ourselves, and the _____ is not in us."

5. Psalms 32:1 says, ""Blessed (fortunate) is he whose transgression is _____, whose sin is _____.""

6. We need to _____ those who offend us, just as God also forgives me.

7. According to Matthew 18:21-22, how many times are we to forgive others every day, including our enemies?

   _____

8. According to Mark 3:29-30, which is the only sin that God can't forgive? The _____ against the Holy Spirit.

9. 1 John 1:9 says that if we _____ our sins, God is faithful and just to _____ us and _____ us from all unrighteousness."

10. According to the chapter, forgiveness is one of the fruits of true _____.

8

PRAYING IS TALKING TO GOD

When we pray, we open our hearts to God and tell Him how we feel.

Praying, or talking to God, is very simple.

I am going to share some tools from God's own Word, the Bible, to make your prayers more powerful and effective.

In **Matthew 6:9-13**, we find our model prayer, also known as 'The Lord's Prayer.' *It was Jesus' reply to his disciples when they asked Him, "Lord, teach us how to pray to the Father?"*

THE LORD'S PRAYER

9 In this manner, therefore, pray:
"Our Father in heaven, hallowed be Your name.
10 Your kingdom come.
Your will be done,
on earth as it is in heaven.

11 Give us this day our daily bread.
12 And forgive us our debts, as we forgive our debtors.
13 And do not lead us into temptation,
but deliver us from the evil one.
For Yours is the kingdom
and the power
and the glory forevermore.
Amen."

We can identify several main points in this prayer:

- In verse 9 we find the Father's dwelling place: The Father is in Heaven.
- The second part of verse 9 is about recognizing the Holiness of His name, for He is Holy.
- To ask that "His kingdom come" means: may everything available in God's Kingdom be brought down into my life and my environment.
- For example, may His love, peace, joy, health, provision, and every Kingdom blessing be established in my life.
- May His will alone be done in my life. May He take control of everything and manage every one of my decisions. May everything be done on earth just as it is done in Heaven.
- In Heaven, only our Father's perfect will is ever done. There is no war, poverty, lack, sorrow, sickness, or death in Heaven.
- In Heaven, everything is filled with glory. It's a glorious manifestation of His vast power and great love.
- Verse 11 says: Give us this day our daily bread. Through this statement, we ask our Heavenly Father to provide us with everything we need for our daily life.
- Let my home never lack any food, nor my family ever be without the most essential items for living, such as our

bread. May our daily food requirements and all of our needs be supplied.

- We can also extend our prayer request for the hungry, sick, and those living on the street, as well as for the orphan and widow. May they never lack any food.

The prayer also speaks to us about forgiveness.

- Verse 12 urges us to ask God for forgiveness for our shortcomings and debts, as we repent for all the times we have failed Him and the things we should have done for Him but didn't.

Remember that asking for forgiveness means repenting for our misdeeds and mistakes.

- Notice that Jesus' model prayer teaches us to align ourselves first with our Heavenly Father. Then, once we have asked for forgiveness, we must forgive ourselves and those who have failed, offended, deceived, betrayed, or abused us.

- Unforgiveness blocks God's personal blessing of forgiveness in our lives.

In verse 12, Jesus teaches us the importance of forgiveness before we pray and to settle our accounts with everyone we come in contact with so we can be in right standing with God.

- We must not hold grudges or hate anyone, no matter how bad they have been. If we genuinely want to enter into a life of prayer and fellowship with the Father, we must learn to forgive.

Once again, here's a tip to remember: If I want God to forgive me, I need to forgive all my debtors who have waged war against me and my own. Only then will we pray and be heard.

TEMPTATION

Verse 13 ends with Jesus saying, "Lead us not into temptation, but deliver us from evil."

- A more accurate translation of the original text leaves no doubt whatsoever that knowing God's divine, holy, and pure nature and that we are His children, He will never set up temptations to trap us.

If we were to paraphrase the line, it would look like this: Good Father, keep me or us from falling into temptation. Keep us from sinning further and deliver us from evil or from doing what is wrong.

PRAISE AND GLORY TO GOD ALONE!

The last part of verse 13 says: "...For Yours is the kingdom and the power and the glory forevermore. Amen."

- We must always thank God for His power and glory when we pray. We must always recognize that everything comes from Him, is in Him and for Him, and that nothing belongs to us. We also confess that all the glory belongs to the Father exclusively, forevermore.

- The last part of the prayer teaches us to ask the Father to deliver us from boasting whenever He blesses us bountifully. May He always help us remember that everything we do is by His great power and grace, guidance and wisdom, as well as the grace of His most powerful Holy Spirit.

Psalms 5:3
"My voice You shall hear in the morning, O Lord;
In the morning I will direct it to You and wait on You."
This is how David prayed.

- Each one of us must pray to the Father in our own words, as his precious Holy Spirit inspires us.

I pray like this every day:

"Heavenly Father, thank You for this beautiful day You've given us.
We love you. We bless and acknowledge you as our Lord and provider. Let your perfect will be done today and take control of the entire day. Lord,
forgive me for failing you.
Please keep me from falling into temptation,
deliver me, Father.
Teach me to forgive and never harbor any grudges in my heart.
Keep me pure in my entire spirit and soul.
Thank you for being so faithful!
I recognize that all the glory is yours alone, God.
And thank you for every blessing that you already have in store for us.
In Jesus' precious name, we pray.
Amen!"

I will now explain a few other truths and foundations about prayer:

- We must practice prayer and talk with the Father every day and at all times.

1 Thessalonians 5:17 exhorts us to *"Pray without ceasing."*

- Prayer should be spontaneous, just like when you start a new relationship with someone, and more so upon realizing that this person did something great for you.

- Besides, it's the person to whom we owe our lives. We must pray with gratitude in our hearts for all the good things we have received from Him and the incredible promises and blessings He showers over our life.

When we talk about different types of prayers, we can classify them in a myriad of ways.

- What matters most is that the prayers you raise to Him come from the heart.

God's word gives us many different ways and forms to pray. It teaches us how to raise powerful and effective prayers to reach the one we direct them to, our Heavenly Father.

Let us see a few recommendations:
- In the following scripture, we are advised not to pray with vain repetitions:

Matthew 6:7

"And when you pray, do not use vain repetitions as the heathen do. For they think that they will be heard for their many words."

- I recommend using the Word of God when we pray. It is vitally important because this way we will be speaking what God has already said or promised us in His Word.
- Always pray to your Heavenly Father.

Jeremiah 33:3

"Call unto Me, and I will answer you, and show you great and mighty things, which you do not know."

- Pray with thanksgiving.

Philippians 4:6-7

6 "Be anxious for nothing, but in everything by prayer and supplication, with thanksgiving, let your requests be made known to God;
7 and the peace of God, which surpasses all understanding, will guard your hearts and minds through Christ Jesus."

Colossians 4:2 *"Continue earnestly in prayer, being vigilant in it with thanksgiving..."*

Psalms 86:12 *"I will praise You, O Lord my God, with all my heart, and I will glorify Your name forevermore."*

- Praising and worshiping God!

Psalms 66:17 *"I cried to Him with my mouth, and*

He was extolled with my tongue."

- Exalting and Glorifying God.

Psalms 34:3 *"Oh, magnify the Lord with me, and let us exalt His name together."*

Psalms 69:30 *"I will praise the name of God with a song, and will magnify Him with thanksgiving."*

Matthew 11:25 *"At that time Jesus answered and said, "I thank You, Father, Lord of heaven and earth, that You have hidden these things from the wise and prudent and have revealed them to babes."*

- We must pray humbly before the presence of God, acknowledging our condition of guilt or fault.

Let's take a look at how King David prayed in **Psalms 51:1-4,**
1 "Have mercy upon me, O God, according to Your lovingkindness; according to the multitude of Your tender mercies, blot out my transgressions.
2 Wash me thoroughly from my iniquity, and cleanse me from my sin.
3 For I acknowledge my transgressions, and my sin is always before me.
4 Against You, You only, have I sinned, and done this evil in Your sight—that You may be found just when You speak, and blameless when You judge.

- We must pray by coming before God not only with a cleansed and contrite heart but also with sincerity and integrity.

Matthew 6:5-6

5"And when you pray, you shall not be like the hypocrites. For they love to pray standing in the synagogues and on the corners of the streets, that they may be seen by men. Assuredly, I say to you, they have their reward.
6 But you, when you pray, go into your room, and when you have shut your door, pray to your Father who is in the secret place; and your Father who sees in secret will reward you openly."

- We must pray, bringing our needs and requests and all our desire to please Him alone.

Hebrews 10:22 *"Let us draw near with a true heart in full assurance of faith, having our hearts sprinkled from an evil conscience and our bodies washed with pure water."*

Matthew 7:11 *"If you then, being evil, know how to give good gifts to your children, how much more will your Father who is in heaven give good things to those who ask Him!"*

- We must pray always mindful that God listens to a humbled and repentant heart.

Hebrews 4:16 *"Let us therefore come boldly to the throne of grace, that we may obtain mercy and find grace to help in time of need."*

James 4:8 *"Draw near to God and He will draw near to you. Cleanse your hands, you sinners; and purify your hearts, you double-minded."*

- At the end of our prayer time with God, we should thank Him for the answers we know He will grant us.

1 Corinthians 15:57 *"But thanks be to God, who gives us the victory through our Lord Jesus Christ."*

Psalms 34:1-4

1 "I will bless the Lord at all times; His praise shall continually be in my mouth.
2 My soul shall make its boast in the Lord; the humble shall hear of it and be glad.
3 Oh, magnify the Lord with me, and let us exalt His name together.
4 I sought the Lord, and He heard me, and delivered me from all my fears.

- When we pray asking for something, we must believe in faith, for without it, it is impossible to please God.

Matthew 21:22 *"And whatever things you ask in prayer, believing, you will receive."*

- All prayer must be made in Jesus' name because He is the one who opened a way for us to reach the presence of God the Father. Through His sacrifice on the cross, we have entry and direct access to His throne of grace.

John 14:13-14

13 And whatever you ask in My name, that I will do, that the Father may be glorified in the Son.
14 If you ask anything in My name, I will do it.

John 15:7
"If you abide in Me, and My words abide in you, you will ask what you desire, and it shall be done for you."

- We can pray at all times and in any place and position.

Philippians 4:6 reminds us to *"Be anxious for nothing, but in everything by prayer and supplication, with thanksgiving, let your requests be made known to God..."*

- We can stand, approved, before His throne of grace in prayer, with nothing to be ashamed about since we have already come into His presence and repented before the Father. We have been purified as gold and silver, and every impurity has been removed from our lives.

2 Timothy 2:14-16 encourages us to:
15 "Be diligent to present yourself approved to God, a worker who does not need to be ashamed, rightly dividing the word of truth.
16 But shun profane and idle babblings, for they will increase to more ungodliness."

- The apostle Paul uses the phrase: To present ourselves before God "approved."

- The word approved means good, satisfactory, well, and sufficient. It implies that we have already repented and asked for the Father's forgiveness.

- Approved means that we no longer have anything to make us feel ashamed before God because we have already been completely forgiven.

- Approved: to stand confidently before God; with words of truth, not feigned, sincere and pure words, not vulgar or vain; words that are pleasing to the Lord.

QUESTIONNAIRE

Exercise 1: Read each Bible verse and fill in the blanks with the correct answers.

1) Psalms 5:3 says, "My _____ You shall hear in the morning, O Lord;

In the _____ I will direct it to You, and I will look up.

2) Matthew 6:10 says, "Your _____ come. Your will be done on earth as it is in _____.

3) Another word for talking to God is _____.

4) According to Matthew 6:7, whenever we pray, we must avoid using _____.

5) Philippians 4:6 and Colossians 4:2 says that we must pray with and be vigilant to our answers to prayer with:_____

6) According to 1 Thessalonians 5:17, how often should we pray?_____

On the blank, write the Bible passage that mentions the following characteristics about prayer:

7) "Give us this day our daily bread.":

_____

8) We must come boldly before the throne of God in prayer:

_____

9) Be anxious for nothing but in prayer and supplication, with thanksgiving, let your requests be made to God:

_____

10) Draw near to God and He will draw near to you:_____

Exercise 2: Write the correct word or Bible passage from the box to complete each statement:

Psalms 51:1-4	Matthew 6:7
Philippians 4:6	Psalms 66:17
Matthew 18:19-20	Psalms 145:1-4

1. Prayers of praise and exaltation:_____

2. "I cried to Him with my mouth:_____

3. Do not use vain repetitions:_____

4. Where two or more agree concerning anything in prayer:

   _____

5. Be anxious for nothing, but bring your needs unto God in prayer: _____

6. Have mercy on me Oh God and cleanse me from my sin:

   _____

Answers

OUR HEAVENLY FATHER

Exercise 1:

1) formed, covered, womb.
2) eyes, fashioned
3) bastards, orphans, children
4) formed, womb, prophet
5) man, image

Exercise 2:

1) Yahweh
2) Elohim
3) Shaddai
4) Adonai
5) Elyon

Exercise 3:

1) God.
2) Christ Jesus
3) Omnipresent
4) Omnisicient
5) Omnipotent.
6) Holy.
7) Hosts.
8) AM WHO I AM.

JESUS CHRIST

Exercise 1:
1) birth.
2) death, resurrection.
3) world, son, everlasting
4) reputation, bondservant
5) born, Holy Spirit
6) lamb, sin
7) price, cross.
8) love, life.
9) died, abundantly
10) life
11) heart, died
12) save
13) free
14) death
15) sickness.
16) victory.

THE HOLY SPIRIT

Exercise 1:
1) pray, helper.
2) a) teach us all things.
   b) bring to remembrance all things.
3) Upper room, 120 people.
4) Acts.
5) power, witnesses.

Exercise 2:
1) Ephesians 4:12-15
2) John 16:13
3) Romans 8:26
4) 2 Corinthians 1:4

5) 1 John 2:27
6) Acts 1:8
7) 1 John 5:12
8) Romans 5:5
9) John 16:8
10) 2 Corinthians 3:17
11) Mark 13:11
12) Romans 8:11
13) 1 Corinthians 12:1-12

WATER BAPTISM

Exercise 1:

1) immersed in water
2) Matthew 28:19-20
3) immersed in Christ
4) filled with power
5) repentance
6) public witness
7) John 3:15
8) Christ
9) baptized
10) cannot enter the Kingdom of God

THE LORD'S SUPPER

Exercise 1:

1) bread, body, cup, covenant
2) drink, proclaim, death
3) As often as we want.
4) bread, wine

5) examine yourself.

6) weak, sick, sleep.

7) Jesus Christ's DNA is in the wine / healing in our body

REPENTANCE

Exercise 1:

1) Repentance.

2) Mouth, heart.

3) Lord

4) Sin

5) Forgiveness.

6) Faithful, forgive

7) There is a celebration.

8) Sins, confesses, forsakes.

9) Forever.

10) Forgive.

FORGIVENESS

Exercise 1:

1) snow

2) heart, spirit.

3) full.

4) deceive, truth.

5) forgiven, covered.

6) forgive.

7) seventy times seven.

8) blasphemy

9) confess, forgive, cleanse

10) repentance.

PRAYER

Exercise 1:
1) voice, morning
2) kingdom, heaven.
3) prayer.
4) vain repetitions.
5) thanksgiving.
6) at all times or without ceasing.
7) Matthew 6:11.
8) Hebrews 4:16
9) Philippians 4:6
10) James 4:8

Exercise 2:
1) Psalms 145:1-4
2) Psalms 66:17
3) Matthew 6:7
4) Matthew 18:19-20
5) Philippians 4:6
6) Psalms 51:1-4

Afterword

*Thank you for allowing me to accompany you on this
first step of your discipleship journey.
Never forget that Jesus is the only way to God!
And with Him in your life, all things are possible because
there's nothing we can do without Him.
Until our next discipleship meeting,
May God richly and bountifully bless you!*

Maritza Rivera